Little Bit Of Everything

Regarding to almost every aspect of life

Urvashi Sinha

ISBN 978-93-5458-564-7
© Urvashi Sinha 2021
Published in India 2021 by Pencil

A brand of

One Point Six Technologies Pvt. Ltd.
123, Building J2, Shram Seva Premises,
Wadala Truck Terminal, Wadala (E)
Mumbai 400037, Maharashtra, INDIA
E connect@thepencilapp.com
W www.thepencilapp.com

Author biography

Just a Simple and normal person who want to make a little change! Even though a little but meaningful change.

CONTENTS

Epigraph

To All Those Lost Souls Who Have Forgotten To Believe In The Immensity Of Love, Hope, Passion, Belief, And Life!
(DEDICATION's INSPIRATION CAME FROM ONE TREE HILL. SO CREDIT GOES !)

Introduction

First of all, this book as it appears ... isn't meant to be a heavy read. As people must have heard this saying many times that 'quality over quantity. I want my readers to read and get as much as possible in a short span of time. I hope and tried my level best to provide what I wrote above! On an honest note, I always wanted to provide the majority of people something extremely meaningful, something that matters, something that can provide some meaning and value to some people who feel kind of lost, who are searching that could really make sense in everyone's life out there! I have decided to provide all those valuable, meaningful thoughts in a form of a book. And that something, that almost everyone could apply in their own practical life. By the way, not to mention that this is my first ever book altogether. I believe in the power of words, so that is why I have decided to write this book.

Hope you all enjoy this book. And most importantly everyone could get something valuable out of this book, anything but something.

Author: Urvashi Sinha

With Regards To My Readers
- Love Urvashi

To get in touch with the Author -
Author's Contact Info :
Email: sinhaurv@gmail.com
Instagram Handle (Personal): @sinhaurv

Instagram Official Handle: @21littlebitofeverything
Twitter Handle: @urv97

Power Of Words

 Sometimes words can work as an energy drink! Funny right? But what's really interesting is that it is true at the same time. Sometimes or most of the time words work so much more than we could expect from them. We need to choose the right words not just for others but for ourselves too! Words are essential simply because we communicate through words. the responsibility of using the right words at the right time is a responsibility that usually relies on human beings as we do have not just one but so many different languages, tounges, a hell lot of a vocabulary that is so immense and deep as an ocean.

Sometimes words work like a support system. Words are an essential part of our life. Words can win hearts and on the contrary of that, they can break hearts too!

And to take note of this, words often or maybe most of the time can hurt people than any injury because words cause injury directly to the heart! People may have heard this that words cannot be taken back but my thought on this is that if you can't take the words back you think you shouldn't have said, then at the least, you can cover those words by saying words you should have said! Do not hesitate in saying the right words ever! Words can make or break any relationship. You are responsible for what you say, then you should be responsible for what you should say too! And always remember it's never too late! Also to remember that your words show what lies in your heart, even if u say it in anger or something you don't mean but still words always at last show the depth of your heart to the person right next to you, whether you actually meant it or not! Now let's talk about how you should use words to yourself!

Every day say motivational words to yourself that no one is willing to say to you!

Believe that you yourself and your words are the biggest strength to you.

Listening to words coming from anywhere, remind you of

something that you might have forgotten. That is also why words are essential.

They remind you or make you think something you never thought of. So my lovely readers keep saying beautiful and meaningful words to us and to others as well. Make words strengths not weaknesses.

You Have Something Inside You

First things first, never take yourself for granted. In other words, never underestimate your worth! The time you do this to yourself, others will automatically do the same with you. The most important point here is, as the title says 'You have something inside you. The matter is, some people cannot identify their 'something' part for their entire life. Every single person on this planet has their own worth, quality, maybe talent too. In this world of increasing unemployment, we need to discover ourselves more than ever! It just takes little discovery, exploring. For examples or the little reference, you can read the further chapters. Never stop believing that you have something, you are something! These things might feel like philosophical to some people, maybe to many people but these philosophical things turn out to be logical ones only if you apply them. I, myself don't believe in philosophy until they are logical in a true manner! Never stop believing in 2 important aspects 1. Time, as time makes many things clear, time heals, time brings out opportunities as well. 2nd but most important is you yourself, simply because at the end of the day you yourself is the only key solution, because as I mentioned this in one of the other chapters of this book that nothing and no one could be the solution of any of your problems in a permanent
Manner (Things and people work

Effectively in your life, but not for the rest of your life as you are the only person in this whole world who is going to be there for your own self for the rest of your life no matter what! Eventually the permanent solution is you yourself. Believe me, belief works wonder along with patience of course! It cannot be possible that any person doesn't have anything inside them.

In a rare scenario where this might happen that you are not able to find that 'Something' then it's time to make something out of nothing. It means do, try your hand in different-different kind of things until you find that 'Something' within you out of nowhere. To make something, find something out of nothing is a pretty difficult task but not impossible and it becomes essential when needed like this, because at the end of the day you have to find that 'Something' within you, no matter what. No one can bring out that thing from you but you, yourself can! We know ourselves more than anyone right!

Love something, get interested, get indulged, get inclined, get passionate about something in life in a way that you will find yourself and you will find that 'Something'. Also let me make it another thing clear that it is not essential for everyone to be superior, have some special trait, to be excellent in any skill. This Chapter's main purpose is to make people understand that they cannot be unworthy or invaluable (As some people almost have no trait or skills within themselves) the thing is that we all human beings are valuable and worthy somewhere for something or for someone. The value of any person doesn't get defined by his/her accomplishments, success or failure. Just think that as human beings we could be of help to anyone, which kind of help or support depends on person- to- person. This is the biggest value of a person to be useful to someone or something, and most important is that we all have this value within ourselves no matter how we look, what work we do, what are our accomplishments in life or what is our identity in this world. Usefulness is the biggest trait, value and accomplishment. And this is what makes us all worthy in an equal manner. So from today on, never, ever take your own value for granted or underestimate your own worth. Whoever you are and wherever you are, remind yourself that you do matter, you are something & you have something.

Life Is Mixture Of Taking And Giving

I have read an amazing article or blog post by Darius Foroux many days ago (You can find his article on medium.com website) the title of that article was "The purpose of life is not happiness' and the article tries to tell us that pursuit of happiness is endless, it simply means that one day we do something that makes us feel happy and then the next day we again start looking for something that could make us feel happy again. And eventually the main message of that article was that the purpose of life is being useful to someone or if possible to many! The article's focus was on usefulness. How we as people should focus on doing something in life that matters to someone that could impact someone's life. In short you should lead a meaningful life. The article also tells us that when we do something to make ourselves happy whether it is being in a relationship and getting love, going for shopping, going for holiday etc… We basically consume things and we don't create things that could mean to someone. Well the best part of that article I found was that it tells us that to do something meaningful in life doesn't mean you have to change the world or something like that, it also could be simple and small things that could make things easy for someone, that could make someone happy or bring smile on their face (examples are given in the article). To bring little change in someone's life, to do something meaningful, we don't need to be a superhero or something like that. Life is a mixture of give and take. We can't always be content if we do only one out of those, be it only giving or only taking. People who only take for their entire life, are left alone eventually or are not able to make a small special place in someone's heart or life. we are living beings, we are human beings so no matter how great at heart we are or how kind we are just like we have and had some amazing great people in our world who almost for their entire life done something for a large group of people be it Mother Teresa

Mother Teresa Or Mahatma Gandhi Ji

Well people like them are one in a billion, but as normal or usual human beings no matter how kind we are at heart still, every once in a while we would feel the need to consume care, love, or something that we love, rather than just giving these things to others! In short, life is and if it is not it should be about living for yourself as well as for others. It's all about balance I think. Very few people might say that we should live only for others or dedicate our life to others just like some of the greatest personalities ever did. The only thing I might wonder for a saying like this is that if we decide to do everything for others (just suppose) and if we don't do the things we enjoy, we love to do, which makes us happy, then in which life we would do these things! We only have one life right. In short, when the time comes when we would be taking our last breaths, make sure that we lived a life worth living or it could be like this too 'your life was worth lived' just this single thought is enough to make all the sense in the world. Anyways I am going to share the link to that article which I was talking about in the beginning, here it is:

https://medium.com/dariusforoux/the-purpose-of-life-is-nothappiness-its-usefulness-65064d0cdd59

You can check the article here on the above link:
Also sharing screenshots that include some incredible lines from a worth watching short meaningful video:

The cancer diagnosis came too late
to give me at least a tenuous hope for a long
life, but I realized that the most important
thing abut death is to ensure that you leave
this world a little better than it was before
you existed with your contributions.

The way I've lived my life so far,
my existence or more precisely the loss of it,
will not matter because I have lived without
doing anything impactful.you existed
with your contributions.

We care so much about the health and integrity
of our body that until death, we don't notice
that the body is nothing more than
a box – a parcel for delivering our personality,
thoughts, beliefs and intentions to this world.

If there is nothing in this box that
can change the world, then it doesn't matter
if it disappears. I believe that we
all have potential, but it also takes a lot of
courage to realize it.

Leave a mark in this world.
Have a meaningful life, whatever definition
it has for you. Go towards it.
The place we are leaving is a beautiful
playground, where everything is possible.
Yet, we are not here forever.

Our life is a short spark in this
beautiful little planet that flies with incredible
speed to the endless darkness of the
unknown universe. So, enjoy your time
here with passion.
Make it interesting. Make it count!

Obsession Of People With Biological Child

Every couple in this world wants their own child, let me clear their own BIOLOGICAL child and not just a child. Some people in this world take care of their pets' dogs and cats etc... Like their own child, but the same kind of people want their human child to be biological.

There could be emotions behind this but there is no logic behind wanting to have your own biological child. What my understanding says about this want of people (Without any kind of research) this is all because of emotions, obsession, and self-satisfaction. Very recently before started writing this, I saw a very long article in 'The Times Of India' about some people in India who want the environmental & climate kind of well needed changes before creating another human who will have to face the harshness of the environment. In fact, some of them are totally denying having a child of their own because they think that there are millions of humans & animals as well who are in need of getting accepted or getting completely owned.

Their philosophy is purely simple and logical too that why create new ones and creating problems for them when there are already humans and animals out there who are facing the harshness of not being owned. Why not become the solution to someone rather than creating more humans for facing problems. Of course, the beauty of that feeling is beyond the words that you get when you have your own biological child.

But to become someone's solution for a lifetime
And to become someone's shining light in their darkness is also a feeling beyond words, both of the feelings cannot be compared. I want people to understand that there are Already many people in this world surviving who need a shoulder to lean on.

Don't create more survivors, and if you really want then first try to solve the existing ones before creating the new ones. At the end of the day, this is all a matter of choice, the understandings and logic can only be given. It is of more importance now to focus more on creating or making a better world, healthier world for our future generations. Personally, I feel a little bit of anger towards the kind of people who have absolutely no idea about their own life or future life but still, they are insistent on having their own 1, 2 or even 3 Children. To produce, to create a life is a big deal, like hell you have to get prepared, get assured that you can take care and take the responsibility of one or more life along with your own!

100% assurance is needed, and if the assurance is not 100% then don't prepare to make a mess out of life, don't prepare to destroy a beautiful life. If you really are hell-bent on wanting to have your own child then get assured, get prepared mentally, physically, emotionally, and financially as well. The responsibility of taking care of a child, of life, should never be taken for granted. It's a huge responsibility, according to which you will have to become a hugely responsible person. Having a child of our own is the most beautiful feeling for every couple, and this feeling can't get compared to any other feeling in this world. But always remember 'The Bigger the Beauty of a Feeling, The Bigger the Responsibility'. I would like to conclude by saying that The beauty of making someone else a part of your life just like you do what you do with your own child is also a beautiful feeling and a beautiful responsibility, to save and make someone else's life! All you gotta do is to give it a chance.

I HOPE YOU ALL ENJOYED READING THIS!

Change! How, When And Why

Everyone is aware of the fact that change is important for the growth of life. Change is indeed an extremely beautiful part of life! We as human beings have come a long way to the road of growth,

Development, progress through change.

Change makes us far more productive & progressive than ever! We have to make sure that whatever the change is, it Should be progressive and not regressive.

Change should change anything for the better. Change is a beautiful gift that we can give to ourselves as well as to others. Whenever you feel from the

Inside that, it's time to change it then you should without any doubt. It could be anything from a change of our activities, the way we do a certain thing, our Perspective, views, ideologies, and so on! This whole topic of change reminds me of one of my favourite quotes and it is by one Of my favourite international artists Zayn Malik

> *"There comes a day when you realize turning the page is the best feeling in the world, because you realize there is so much more to the book than the page you were stuck on."*
>
> - Zayn Malik

I honestly can't think of a life without change. But still, there are some things in life which are better left unchanged, forever. These kinds of things are not certain, it depends on person to person & life to life.

What I mean to say is that not everything in life needs to be changed every once in a while or maybe forever. We have to make balance in change just like we have to make balance in everything else. Never fear change also at the same time, don't overdo it! Here comes another aspect of change that 'The Bigger The Thing, The Bigger The Difficulty To Change It'. For instance, if it's a thing in your closet or an outfit in your wardrobe it is not of much thinking to change it or not but when it comes to changing ways to get to a certain profession or totally change your biggest dream of life, it is difficult to just think about changing it like hell! Sometimes, change automatically happens in our life and sometimes we are aware of the changes which are not automatic in nature. Well obviously I am not here to give the definition, but what is its meaning in life and how important it is, we need to understand that by our own instinct and understanding. The topic of change reminds me a beautiful song named the same by Charlie Puth, I would like to share it with all my readers!

Listen to Change by Charlie Puth. If any certain change is not doing well for you as you expected, you are feeling unable to cope with it, trying too hard to be comfortable within that change but getting affected in a not so good way then you should know it's time to make that change unchanged .

There Is Purpose Meaning & Beauty Of Life Everywhere

As far as I think, this might be a long chapter compared to others. But I'll try my best to keep it short. I must say that I am going to enjoy a lot writing this, as much as I want my readers to enjoy this. Let's start, there is absolutely no definite purpose, meaning, or beauty of life. Depends upon person to person. Some people think that we can find love only in our girlfriend or boyfriend, spouse. But this is not the only option, actually, we can find real love in anyone and anywhere! It could be our lifetime best friend, it could be our closest relative too, our most lovable pet, our child (it could be an adopted child too), our work (sometimes it happens that our work environment becomes our life & family) and so on! In life, there is no definite definition of purpose and happiness. Make a goal in life and try to achieve it, remember it might be anything. Try to do social work like to help a certain group of people, doing something for animals or having them by yourself and take care of them, make a career goal of getting into a certain profession, Learning and mastering a new skill, believe me, anything like these could become the meaning of your life, the purpose of your life without you even knowing it!

If you are not financially that much strong, that could be your motive too in life, to become financially strong. If you take a close look at life, you will find that there is actually no end of purpose in life. Once, a famous Indian yogi and author Sadhguru said an extremely wonderful, beautiful thing regarding the purpose of life as someone asked him that what is or should be the purpose of life ….he said 'that is the beauty of life that there is no definite purpose!' He said what if there had been a definite purpose of life and when we fulfill that after that we would kind of wander around thinking what should we do now. Well, I really liked his answer. as to what the conclusion we have out of that is that having found your purpose is great…but also if you haven't found it yet there should be no worry for that, it's ok….take it easy….at the end of the day it's just life.

Purposes could be like desires, a never-ending process. So enclosing I would like to say, find your own purpose in life and
Cherish it and nurture it with passion.

Do let me know that what purpose in life you have found, if possible!

THE PURPOSE OF LIFE
IS LIVING A LIFE
OF PURPOSE.

Be Positive Be Happy

I simply find no sympathy for people who get sad or are sad most of the time because of such small things or maybe no things at all! I don't understand that for some people why it is so difficult to be happy, chill even when everything is almost okay in their life.

Well still I would like to share the solutions to these kind of people too! Being busy is the easiest, instant and most effective way of dealing with unnecessary depressiveness, laziness and not being happy at all kind of feel. Simplest solution is being busy in anything good or anything worth being busy in! Get indulge in activities it could be falling in love too! Anything which keeps you busy and indulged. Fall in love, if possible do social work, spend time with your pets, learn something new and so on!

There are so many things that could help you with that unnecessary sadness or depressiveness. Don't think about anything too much. Don't get serious on small things like someone said something to you or anything like this. It's your life which only comes for once, try to live it to the fullest possible. People actually don't need motivation daily, they are just habitual of that. Think that we are mature and intelligent and intellectual enough to motivate

& inspire ourselves daily, if nothing is there for you to do the same there is always reasons for simplest thing which is happiness, you just have to find that a little. Speaking of happiness and sadness I would like to mention that I am here to help, it means if any of you who are reading this having some serious problems in life I am here to help. I can give my suggestions and try to help to the fullest of my capabilities, eventually it's up to you what you people do with that suggestion. Honestly, I would love to help according to my capabilities! Before enclosing I want to share some of my very favourite and meaningful quotes -

"So I've been thinking about this
whole being happy thing, & I feel
like people get lost when they think
of happiness as a destination...
we're always thinking that someday
we'll be happy; we'll get that car
or that job or that person in our lives
that'll fix everything.
But happiness is a mood,
& it's a condition, not a destination.
It's like being tired or hungry,
it's not permanent.
It comes and goes, & that's okay.
And I feel like if people thought of it
that way, they'd find happiness more often."
- One Tree Hill

ONE TREE HILL

One of my most favorite

Padne layak kuch likh jao ya, likhne layak kuch kar jao By Dr. APJ. ABDUL KALAM JI (ENGLISH. write something worth reading or do something worth writing about!)

A SKILL LEARN IS A SKILL EARN

Be skill full! And why not? In today's digital world learning has become so easy. Whenever we learn something new, even if it is a small thing, it feels like an achievement. So why is it important to learn new things? Some people might wonder that! Some people might think like this because perhaps they have a great future ahead of them like some would become or are successful doctors,

lawyers, engineers,
entrepreneurs, etc. People might think that why we should waste time. Well like I said
in my previous articles as well, there is always time for everything, depending upon the priorities.

Learning new skills simply gives you a high confidence level, might get you earning as well. Also to take notice of this that sometimes or some people have some skills inborn, then, in this case, we have to polish that particular skill. There is no doubt by saying this that learning a skill, any skill, can never get wasted. People get to know the importance of learning any skill throughout the time or maybe when the right time comes. Some people are gifted with skills by birth not to mention that is a wonderful thing. But if someone doesn't have any kind of skill automatically, they can simply try their hands on some skills and later can decide whether they are good at that or not. Some people have to find out their skills, they need to discover what they are good at, from which skill they can get benefited or vice versa. Skills can benefit us in many ways and in a long run. All you have to do is just develop those, or nurture them (if you are gifted). At the very least the skills learned to give us satisfaction, make us feel good and confident more than ever before! Once Bollywood Actor Hrithik Roshan was speaking about his parenting ways in an Interview that 'he let his sons try on their hands in different- different kind of things so that they can discover in what they are good and that might lead them to Discover their passion or maybe profession as well. This is a famous saying that learning doesn't stop in our entire life that is a natural learning process.

NOTE: LEARN ANYTHING BUT SOMETHING.

In this digital age we can't make an excuse, we can learn anything we want and what's really interesting is that most of them are free of cost to learn. Sometimes we can't recognize what kind of privileges we do have. We can only identify its importance when we see places where learning for people is an alien thing. So do learn something if you too have that privilege. And always remember that learning is never, ever going to be a waste of time & energy! It will provide you something or other.

PUTTING A L BEFORE EARNING, WILL MAKE IT EASIER! - Urvashi

You Cannot Have It All At Once

Before people misunderstand, I am going to write all negative let me make it clear that 'You can have it all, but not at once'. In this world people run for making a stable career, on the other hand they run for making a family or maybe just to have their own love life, all at the same time. What happens to this is that they end up neither making a great stable career for themselves nor to able to increase the quality of their personal life ! People should not be in a rush. These things demand quality of time and dedication at the same time. Or let's just say that it's all a matter of time! Leaving the exceptions behind, as there are all kinds of exceptions in this world. While childhood we study, play and maybe learn something too. We can never make a career in childhood, even if someone tries to do that, they will surely get failed. Well there are 2 major points I am talking about, first there is a certain time for everything whether its studies, professional career or having a family. If people try to get anything before its actual time, there are 99% chances they will get failed at it, will not be able to handle it. Second major point is that don't try to get all the things you want to get, in a short period of time.

Because as I said it before you will get fail. Just like every time I say this considering that I am a

huge movie lover, let's understand this simple point

through a simple dialogue from movie 'Ye jawaani hai deewani'.

We don't need to set a bunch of things, especially when we know we can't get this much done..especially in a short span of time! We just need to set 1 or
maybe 2 essential career goals, 1 personal life goal (it could be marrying someone and having kids or maybe according to circumstances being single and adopting a kid) it could

be anything depending upon who are you, what are your present circumstances etc..! Now you need to prioritize what you need to do first, like for instance getting strong financially usually gets to be the first priority because only then you can take care of your personal life right! But like I said before all these goals and priorities in life depends on person to person. Also never forget a very important thing is that after setting up a priority, never ever regret your set of priorities even if you have to. Let's make it simple for people to understand with a little example. 'Imagine you choose To first give priority to your career and at the same time someone proposed you and you turned down that offer OR you can imagine it vice versa.

There is a possibility that in future because of circumstances you might regret your choices'. Never ever regret your choices. Because no matter how hard you try or how many ways or how many options you try, eventually people regret something or other. Regret the things you have done wrong, not the things you have just done! Because when it comes to choosing one thing over other, prioritising what to choose first….regret is going to come most likely ! Regret is just an emotion, feeling in human beings just like sadness, anger, happiness, satisfaction.

Life Is All About Balance

How to have a balance in life? And what are the ways to have it in life? Now, this is obvious that for some people work and money is more important, some people never get serious towards their professional career or even towards earning a little amount of money. But truth is we should not take anything for granted. Because if we do so, it is reasonable that we will not get successful in that particular thing.

Seriously, I don't know if I should write this obvious thing or not. But as always on This particular 'Obvious' topic, I want to share my understanding & my own thoughts. Well, having a balanced life is about a great time management. Followed by a great understanding of priorities. Of course I can't write down a time table of an ideal daily routine or a few lines about time management because of course that will make no sense. Because having a balance in life depends on person to person. There are different kind of time management schemes work for different kind of people. I can only share my understanding or viewpoint about management & balance in life! People just need to understand and remember a few points. Just like I said before, don't take anything for granted weather its professional life or personal. Spending time with friends & family is as important as spending time with yourself too.

Work is important for a living but at the same time, life is all about living your kind of dreams and collecting memories. Some people get stressed out or even get into depression. Why? Simply because they are not able to cope with the work requirements, they themselves created. Then they try to pretend like a victim of excessive workload and all. Always remember (If leaving rare circumstances behind) in whichever situation we are right now, has been affected mostly by our own choices. Don't cry over excessive workload or extremely busy life, become responsible for the choices you make and the things you do in your life. Be mature and don't become a so called victim of your circumstances. Be mature enough to make a balance. It's not that difficult a task, it's just a game of priorities and you need to be a smart player enough. Believe in your instincts! If you are unable to cope and make balance between everything, simply decrease the amount of activities according to priorities. And never forget to enjoy the life every once in a while, especially after getting too tired of excessive workload or when you really feel the need!

The Power Of Creative Expressions

I have started watching my long loved show ONE TREE HILL since some months.
When the show went off air, I had to wait a lot and finally found it on internet. Now I can watch this series whenever I want. The point is when and how often I need the want to watch this.

Well sometimes when I need some quality or you can say my favourite kind of entertainment, When I am in stress and need to calm myself down or When I feel the need to get inspired, to get motivated or it could be when I am feeling a little bored (Even though getting bored is not the case ever happens to me, well almost never or most of the time). Well for me, this series is one of the most powerful inspiration & stress buster tool along with music & movies. For anyone else it could be books, outing with friends and family, spending time with pets and so on! But here I am talking about the powerful impact of creative expressions in our life given by human beings itself. If we look into this in a philosophical way we can easily say that because creativeness or art comes from one's heart that is why it connects to our hearts in such a powerful manner! What's really interesting is that we can feel its power and beauty in both ways while enjoying it and also while doing it as ourselves as well. Can you guess what is the most interesting, attractive and beautiful quality of all these creative expressions? It might be quite obvious, it is repeating the moments that we loved whenever and there is no such limit of how many times you can repeat it! Its ability to get repeated whenever possible, is its beauty. If any moment, scene or a specific saying or part of a song (it could be the whole song too) makes you happy, you can repeat it anytime, anywhere and can enjoy it in the same way you had before. Also people like to find happiness in these, even though they don't get happiness in their own life all the time. Why? Considering I am a hard core movie lover I am describing the ans. through a dialogue from one of my favourite movies KAPOOR & SONS, one character says "my book's story is real and its ending is not a happy one because there is no guarantee of happy ending in real life too" character's brother says "that's why we the try to find that happiness in stories."

As far as i think, not to mention this but the power of these art forms are both in nature positive and negetive as well. depends upon the usage manner and also it differs from person to person. many people get infuluenced in an extremely wrong manner. what we consume as people does matter a lot... in the form of books, movies, shows, music and it could be games as well nowadays. if people are immature, consuming negetive things would influence them negatively. Also I may not have done any kind of research regarding any topic but so far as much as I have heard and seen in most cases people got influenced in a wrong manner rather than learning good stuff. as there are good and bad stuff shown in an almost equal manner. so ultimately the power, the affect, the influence cannot be measured and it totally depends upon person to person as to what they consume, how they consume, how they take it or in which manner they apply that into their own life, and maybe not to apply at all. obviously the only point eventually i want to make in here is that try to consume positive, good and happy things as much as possible and do apply some good lessons if those seem applicable to you and your life. there is nothing wrong in consuming some violent or negetive content because there could be a good story behind, but never ever get influenced by bad things. i guess what point I can make here is that the bad or negative things that people do consume are not there to teach you something... those are just there for your entertainment purpose or making money or something of outer purpose and not an inner purpose. but most of the time the positive and good things that you consume are there with all the above intentions like entertainment, making money and all that but it also always comes with a hidden intention to teach you those good things, to help you with something, to make you understand something.

the good intentions are somewhere behind the good things but there are never the bad intentions behind some negative kind of stuff or content. so do enjoy everything that you consume, learn only good things and filter otherwise.

Never forget that these creative expressions that I have been talking about are one of the most beautiful gifts to us as human beings. so consume, use and enjoy them in the right manner.

Glimpses From My Diary

This is kind of part 2 of the previous chapter (The Power Of Creative Expressions)

Currently, I am watching my long-loved TV Series or I should say Series of life lessons 'ONE TREE HILL'. I can't describe how much I love ♥this show & how happy I am to found this again (Thanks to the internet). Although I just said I can't describe but actually at the same time I am describing it
LOL

Well, there are many reasons behind why I love this show so much, why it's a huge part of my life, why it does matter to me so much & why I want to keep this series for the rest of my life. First 1. Stress Buster/Mood relaxer, second 2. It makes me happy. This show actually makes me feel light also positive, if I am already feeling these like positive and all….. It simply increases! 3rd but also very important one is that it teaches me so many things, so many essential life lessons that are essential to keep for the rest of the life! So many relatable characters, relatable emotions, relatable circumstances. Honestly I can't express or maybe somehow I can but what I am talking about is the love & admiration I do have for this show! It doesn't only entertains me like hell, but at the same time it is hell lot of a worth watching because of its amazing life lessons! 9 July 2019

Well, I think to my diary it's pretty much clear now that I am a huge lover & admirer of OTH 🖤 even though I might not get tired writing, praising about it ! Today I am feeling a strong & deep urge to write about my another so very favourite thing, stress buster kum time pass kum favourite entertainer but more than anything my passion….. Watching movies… yeah... It's pretty much my passion! That reminds me how watching cartoons used to be my biggest delight (which is pretty much every kid's delight, kids of my time). With time the hobby of watching movies became my passion! So I guess according to that the title 'A passionate movie lover' would be appropriate for people like me! I also should say this that passionate movie lovers like me, like for us watching movies is a lifestyle. I am very much inclined to many other activities as well but movies are something that I can't resist! Also movies don't only provide me entertainment, happiness but it also provides me some
Important lessons very often! One thing or maybe two are common in movies & OTH (Basically because I am talking about them right now, also mostly) are that both make me laugh when I am not laughing at all, make me happy when I am not at all & so on ….. Make me think, make me feel etc…! I guess, it would not be stupid to say this that things like these are no longer just things because they become friends, sometimes a guide or a teacher …. Simply because of the fact that they make us smile, make us laugh, make us believe …and so on …! So I think all these sayings are enough to mention the importance of these all creative

expressions given by Human Beings! For me 3 most impactful are- Movies, Music & OTH…. And to remind This that this is not in a sequence, anyone of them can beat anyone of them. Cause it all depends on the time. For instance, maybe I am in a situation when I can only listen to the music… It works. Simple!

NOTE: REAL PAGES FROM MY DIARY ARE ON THE NEXT PAGE.

Also currently i am watching my long long loved TV Series or i should say Series of life to lessons 'ONE TREE HILL'. I can't describe how much i love ♥ this show & how happy i am to found this again (Thanx $ to the internet). Although i jus said i can't describe but actually at the same time i am describing it 😄 LOL

Well, there many reasons behind why i love this show so much, why its a huge part of my life, why it does matter to me so much & why i want to keep this series for the rest of my life. First (Number 1.) Stress buster / Mood relexer, Second (Number 2.) It makes me happy. This show actually makes me feel light also positive, if i am already feeling these like positive and all...... it simply increases! 3rd but also very important one is that it teaches me so many things, so many essential ~~life~~ life lessons that are essential

to keep for the rest of the life !
So many realetable charecters, realetable
emotions, realetable circumstances.
Honestly i can't express or maybe
somehow i can, but what i am talking
about is the love & admiration i do have
for this show ! It does'nt only
entertains me like hell, but at the same
time it is hell lot of a worth watching
because of its amazing life lessons !

9 July 2019

Well, i think to my diary its pretty
much clear now that i am a huge
lover & admirer of OTH ♥ Even

though i might not get tired writing, praising about it !

Today i am ~~B~~ feeling a strong & deep urge to write about my another so very fav thing, stress buster Kum Time Pass Kum fav entertainer, but more than anything my passion .... Watching movies .... yeah .. its pretty much is my passion! ~~that~~ That reminds me how ~~watching~~ watching cartoons used to be my biggest delight (which is pretty much every kid's delight, Kids of my time) with time the hobby of watching movies became my passion !

So i guess according to that the title
'A passionate movie lover' would be
appropriate for people like~! I also
should say this that passionate movie
lovers like me, like for us watching
movies is a lifestyle OR is a big part
of the lifestyle. I am very much
inclined to many other activities as
well, but ~~it~~ movies are something that
i can't resist! Also ~~it do~~ movies don't
only ~~too~~ provide me entertainment,
happiness but it also provide me some
important lessons very often!

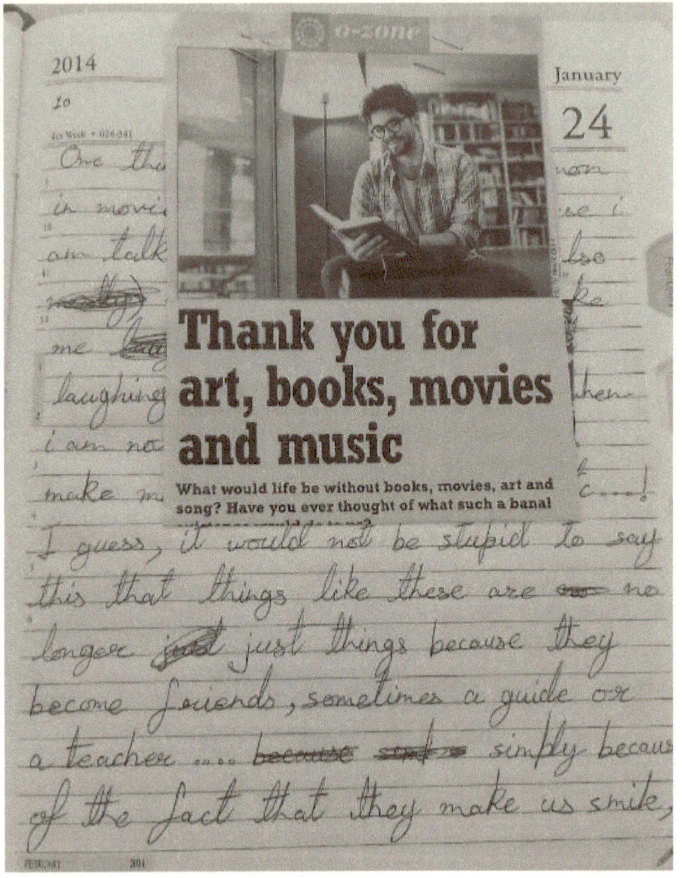

I guess, it would not be stupid to say
this that things like these are no
longer just things because they
become friends, sometimes a guide or
a teacher .... simply because
of the fact that they make us smile,

2014

January

FRIDAY 24

One thing or maybe two are common in movies & OTH (Basically because i am talking about them right now, also ~~mostly~~ mostly) are that Both make me ~~laugh~~ laugh 😄, when i am not laughing at all, make me happy when i am not at all & so on .... make me think, make me feel etc...! I guess, it would not be stupid to say this that things like these are ~~no~~ no longer ~~just~~ just things because they become friends, sometimes a guide or a teacher .... ~~because~~ ~~stuff~~ simply because of the fact that they make us smile, make us laugh, make us believe ... and so on and ...... !

So, i think all these sayings are enough to mention the importance of these all creative expressions given by Human Beings!

For me 3 most impactful are — Movies, Music & OTH ...... and to remember this that this is not in a sequence, anyone anyone of them can beat anyone of them ... Cause it all depends on the time. For instance, maybe i am in a situation when i can only listen the music .. it works. Simple!

The Important Of Being Your Own Best Friend

People need to understand the importance of being their own best friend, because people are not happy within themselves. Being happy and content with nobody but ourselves, is called 'Solitude'. Now let me make it clear that being social or and having relationships of different kind has never been doubted not to be good. So the question that might occur in your mind that why I need to find a friend within myself? When I have amazing people in my life! Well the thought behind it is very simple, there never have been a guarantee of any relationship if it is going to last forever with you or not! It might be any relationship be it a friend, sibling, spouse, or even parents. You need to understand this that you are the only person in this world who is going to be with you, no matter what happens in your life! People need to stop being relied on someone or other to make them happy, content. Now let's say this that we all know being alone is not a justified thing to any human as human beings are social beings from the beginning. But it is worst if you are sad being alone. Now, some people might not understand this totally as some people have never been alone even in an emotional way or some other, they always had someone's back. People like these, who always lives within joint or big family, have their whole family within their city, have decent couple of friends and so on. But not all people are that much fortunate in this sense. Some people are actually alone, especially emotionally. No matter how hard they try not to be alone, but some are meant to be or destined to be alone at least for most of their lives! On the other hand this is also a fact can't be denied that no matter how well you prepare yourself to be content within your own company, every once in a while you need someone no matter what.Which is totally okay, most importantly totally normal. But the point here is to prepare yourself for the times in which you will have nobody but yourself. Trust me when I say this that if you are able to be totally content within your own company, you will never be in a state called 'loneliness', you will be in a state called 'solitude'. Let me give you an amazing example of solitude (as people get more satisfied with examples), this might be a fictional one but trust me this is indeed a great example. I am sure everyone must have seen Mr Bean. And if you haven't watched it yet, you must! This makes me share one of my favourite quotes with all you, which goes like this

(Sometimes the most important thing in life is how to be your own best friend!)

SOMETIMES, THE
MOST IMPORTANT
THING YOU'LL
NEED TO KNOW,
IS HOW TO BE
YOUR OWN BEST
FRIEND.

Let Life, Be Life Not A Race!

In Today's life, most people are living a race, not a life. And when I say this of course most people would be thinking that I am talking about how we always try to compete with our competitors, contemporaries. But here I am not talking about only the competition we do with our contemporaries, but also with ourselves! In today's world parents are making their kids like a machine or to work like a robot. Point to note, here I am not denying the importance of hard work, productivity in life. All I am saying is just not to forget to live for which you are working or maybe studying. In other words, it could be, doing hard work for something or preparing yourself day & night for something, could be studying hard or maybe working on an important project. All these things are essential as this is what makes us move forward in life. If we stop working on something, stop studying hard, stop doing something other productive, or preparing ourselves for something essential, there are 0% chances of us moving forward in life. But my point is simple. Try not to forget to live the life, for which you are doing all these things in your life. If you are not able to get some time to laugh freely, to enjoy some moments once in a while, doing something you really love, spending some time with your loved ones, then for which life you are doing all these efforts, hard work. And by saying this, I am sure you are not doing all these things for your other life (Next Life). In today's time, small kids are achieving so much, making records, getting professional at such a young age. I wonder if they can even think about living life once in a while. All in all, this would make my point perfectly clear 'To have a balanced life. A balance between work lives, personal life, own time, and so on!

The people who today are living like a robot or machine after some time will wonder where life has gone. Life is all about having the proper balance of work, personal life including having a good time with friends and family and also sometimes with ourselves too, learning something new every once in a while, doing what you love to do .. Etc. …! Always try to remember that if you are only working towards making money or getting qualified for some certain profession like engineering or something else, at the same time avoiding or not doing at all things like learning, getting to know something or someone maybe... Your personality might never grow. Because the more you learn new things or skills, the more you read, the more you listen, the more you know, the more you talk (about something good and in a good sense) the more you understand about something or someone (remember it could be anything like getting indulge in some activity like painting, certain topic or thing) the more you grow as a person, as a personality, as an individual! Always remember we study or work to feed ourselves, we nurture relationships to feed our life, and we do things that we love doing to feed our soul! Don't take the 'me time' for granted ever. As this is what makes you, you! We can often make a living out of what we love to do but we can never feed our souls by doing the work, which of course is not able to feed our souls.

Must Read

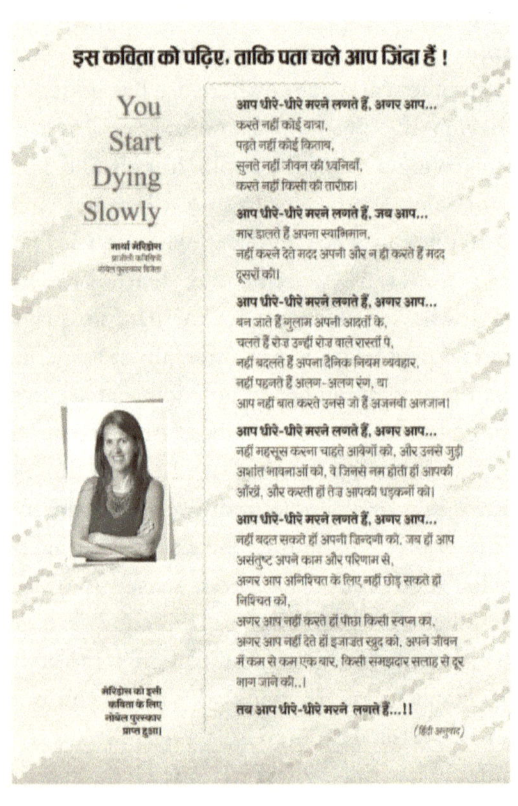

What Is The Measurement Of Life

Life Is Too Long Or Too Short?

Well, the answer to this is extremely simple 'Life is neither short nor long. So how we as humans can measure the length of life! Actually, there is no measurement because life is equal for all of us. If someone lives for 20 years (I wish this doesn't happen to anyone, just for an instance) those 20 years would be equal for everyone who lives for these many years. And this kind of measurement remains the same in all living years examples like if someone lives for 40 years, 60 years, and 90 years and so on! The realization or feeling that we get like sometimes we get a sense as life passing through very slowly, or sometimes we feel that life got passed so quickly that we are not kind of able to believe! Now let's just say that these are just feelings of life measurements and not the actual life measurement as I said before, and as everyone knows that life cannot get measured. This sense or feeling that we get is only because of the difficulty level of our lives. When we go through some tough phases, life seems really very long. And when we go through some very light, happy movements in life…in an extremely obvious manner, life seems like it is getting fly by faster than the time or faster than it should be! Well, there is also an entirely different kind of measurement. I am quite sure that many already must have heard this before that life seems short and fast-paced when we are too young and even when we get adult but as we get extremely older the life automatically seems like a slow-paced journey. Well, the main point or motive to write this article is not to find the measurement of life. My main motive to write over this topic is that should we the people, means us....should we do the things and spend time in life keeping this in mind that life is short or keeping this in mind that life is long and there is always time for anything and everything. Well, I don't know why but whenever I think and write over any kind of topic, eventually and automatically without even trying the conclusion of that particular topic, or discussion comes as balance.

No matter on which topic I am
Thinking over but every important subject of our lives comes across balance or I should say everything that we should do in life in any aspect should get surrounded with balance! Just like that in this topic, I want to conclude my motive by saying that we cannot and should not always keep this in mind that life is long nor should we need to keep this in my that
life is too short always. Now let's get it straight

ALWAYS REMEMBER THAT
NOTHING WORKS IN AN ALWAYS KIND OF A MANNER!

This might means here to say that any kind of ideology cannot always work, in every kind of situation, in every aspect of life! There are always and should be different kind of approaches.

Advises Are Not Always Advises

Yes, you read it right, as advice or suggestions are not always suggestions themselves but most of the time these so-called suggestions are experiences or insecurities indeed. Examples work best, don't they? let's take a close look at one example coming from my own life but it is not mine, it is of one of my friends. a few years ago there is one guy who was and still is a mutual friend of me and my elder sister.

Earlier in his life he always used to say people should never ever waste their time in love ...because there is nothing in this, true love doesn't exist...this, this and that! focus on career only. but then after a year or two, something happened in his life, yes you guessed it right.. Love happened! And when that happened, all of a sudden all his beliefs, ideologies got changed. he started appreciating the love and the of course the girl that he loves! people say what they know so far or sometimes they say things which they may never have experienced themselves but according to what they believe. because we all have certain beliefs and experiences...so for most of the time, people give advice according to these two aspects. Only a few times or let's say rarely it happens that people do give advice according to what they truly think.. could be good or bad for us.

it is up to us that how we come to the conclusion that which advises we should apply over on or say consider over and on which advice we should just ignore...like from hearing in from one side, hearing out from the other. it is a decision just like all kinds of other decisions that we have to considerthrough our wisdom.

We Are Never Too Late

Late for marriage, late for studies, late for business or job, these are some of the thoughts of every average human being but the fact is opposite ' We are never too late for anything. There is no particular time for good things to happen or maybe the right time for the right things to happen. Just like we say that 'Age is just a number' time is also just a number, to which you can count just like we count our age. Let's take a wonderful instance here, suppose one student brings approx... 52% marks in 12th grade at the age of 17 years, after some years at the age of around 25 that student decides to exam again for 12thgrade and this time he/she achieves 88% marks. What do you truly think, bringing out the best ability possible is more essential, or doing the same thing at the appropriate time or earlier is more important. Of course, there is no doubt that we want to see our best ability and capacity to do something not just being at the right time whether it was your best or not! As far as I am concerned satisfaction comes by doing our best capability, our best ability, not by doing earlier or at the appropriate time. In other simple words doing the best is far more important than doing earlier. Time is an illusion, well earlier it was. most of you already know that at the beginning of human existence there was nothing called 'time'. But apparently, to make some disciplined rules or norms to follow through day and night, a thing called 'Time' came into existence, time is made by none other than humans itself. Which totally changed and somehow very much managed human beings ' all activities through day and night. like every penny has its two different sides, the time has too! like if time wouldn't have come, we as humans still be thinking and living free of the thought that time is running but time made us learn how to live or how should we live.

That is why as I mentioned in one of the previous chapters I don't only like but I love the creative expressions so much like movies, music, and books and all because these things don't have the obstacle of time we can live our favorite moments almost whenever we want to! if you have the access to these things don't take them for granted never, ever. The beauty of rewind in those doesn't exist in real life. sometimes it can but most of the time it doesn't.

What Is The Real Meaning Of Solitude

How Should We Acquire Solitude In Life?

What Is The Real Meaning Of Solitude?

Before going to the conclusion, in fact before even start to explore this whole topic, I want to start this subject by declaring the main motive of this whole thing in one single line "AS LIVING BEINGS, ESPECIALLY AS HUMAN BEINGS WE BORN ALONE & DIE ALONE AS WELL. BUT IF OUT OF ANY REASON WE LIVE ALONE TOO, THEN WHAT IS THE DIFFERENCE BETWEEN LIFE & DEATH." Just to clarify that, (In case anyone misunderstood that entire line) here by saying that line I don't mean to say that the only purpose of life is to get together with others. As we all know that human beings are often known as social beings.

Now here is an extremely important note to note down, that as people we have to understand that in life there is no such issue, topic, feeling, or action that doesn't have 2 different sides to it, as I always convey this message of having a balance in every single thing in life by giving the instance of a penny...because penny and everything in life have two different sides. In life there comes the two different sides aspect when we are not having that well-needed balance. Be it anything, if we are giving it lesser time or value than needed then it is considered as neglected, and if we are giving too much importance or time or anything then it is considered an obsession, or less than obsession but of course not in the right manner. having the right balance is a hard thing to pull off in life because then it means to give it the right or appropriate amount of time and value! be it, family, career, personal life, taking care of health, and so on. as I wrote above that having balance is one of the hardest things to pull off in life but at the same time, it is the most essential and well-needed approach as well. well, here in this chapter I am basically talking about the value of solitude which again comes with the right amount of approach.

Well, let's now start by informing that this whole idea or say topic came into my mind after reading an article in THE TIMES OF INDIA'S TIMES LIFE. The whole article in a direct way tells you the importance of self-love, solitude, and how it is possible to live almost alone for the rest of your life & that too in the happiest way possible! What brings me in here out of that article is the disagreement I have with that article, let's just say 80% of disagreement. Not to mention that we are not just living beings but social beings as well. Life is about sharing our life, sharing ourselves. As I mentioned above in the declaration that how every one of us born & dies alone too.., So living alone on purpose doesn't make any sense to me! On the other hand, I am aware of the fact that no one and I mean literally no one wants to live alone on purpose. Solitude is not just a good thing, it's a great thing for anyone who can acquire this. Now there's no doubt in the fact that every one of us..like every single person has their own ideology, own perception regarding life! And in an obvious manner, I am also doing the same, as I am putting down what I think of this whole concept of solitude, more than that of the concept of self-love. I hear and read people giving advice of life, motivating those saying things like…never ever depend on anyone, self-love is everything, there is nothing like true love in this world, and blah..blah and blah….fewww…! Well, as we all know there are always two different sides to every penny (things). Things like self-love and being too damn reserved have a negative side too. It builds a shield around you in such a way that you start being unaware of all the emotions, feelings, that are essential if we want to feel and realize that we are human beings and not robots. As I previously discussed in my previous chapters that there always should be a balance in every kind of thing! And how the extent of anything in life is always going be problematic, disheartening especially the extent of bad things or the things that aren't really necessary. By concluding this chapter I would like to say in short that Solitude is a great thing indeed, but only when it becomes a necessity, it is going to make you survive when there is no one around or something like that. But don't create solitude in your life when it is not needed, trust me.

In short, solitude is an extremely beautiful & a great thing but only when required or needed!

Some Of My Favorite Quotes And Saying

Here i am bringing some of my very favorite quotes and sayings...that matters to me somehow, and somehow i hope all my readers could find the light in these too !

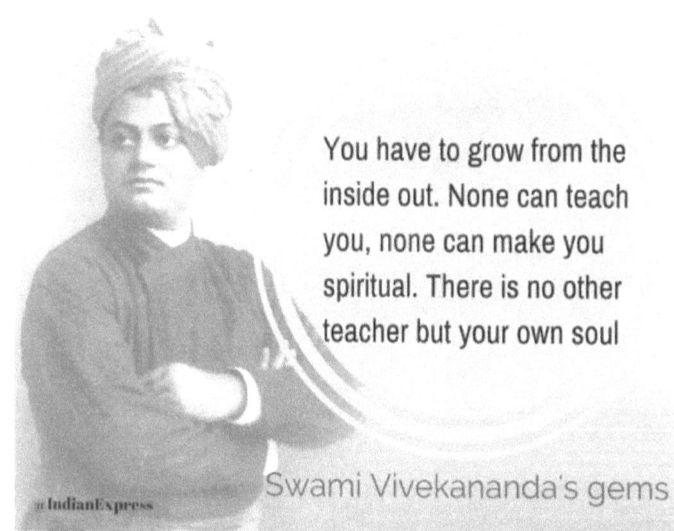

Every single one of us
can play a part
in making the world
a better place.
Take food to a homeless person,
spend an hour with a lonely senior
at a nursing home, help a single
mother with some errands. These
are all little things that make a big
difference.
Play your part.

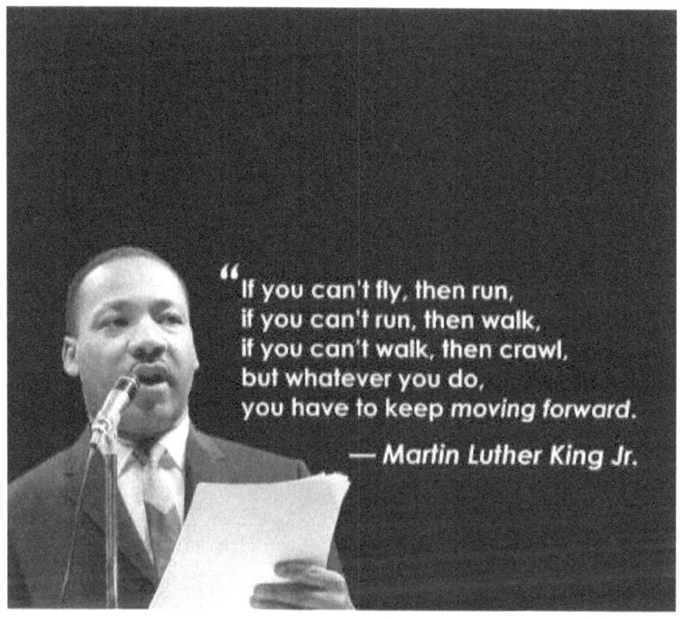
If you can't fly, then run,
if you can't run, then walk,
if you can't walk, then crawl,
but whatever you do,
you have to keep moving forward.

— Martin Luther King Jr.

Never leave a true relation for few faults... Nobody is perfect. Nobody is correct at the end. Affection is always greater than perfection.

PEOPLE DON'T ALWAYS NEED ADVICE.
SOMETIMES ALL THEY REALLY NEED IS
A HAND TO HOLD,
AN EAR TO LISTEN,
AND A HEART TO UNDERSTAND THEM.

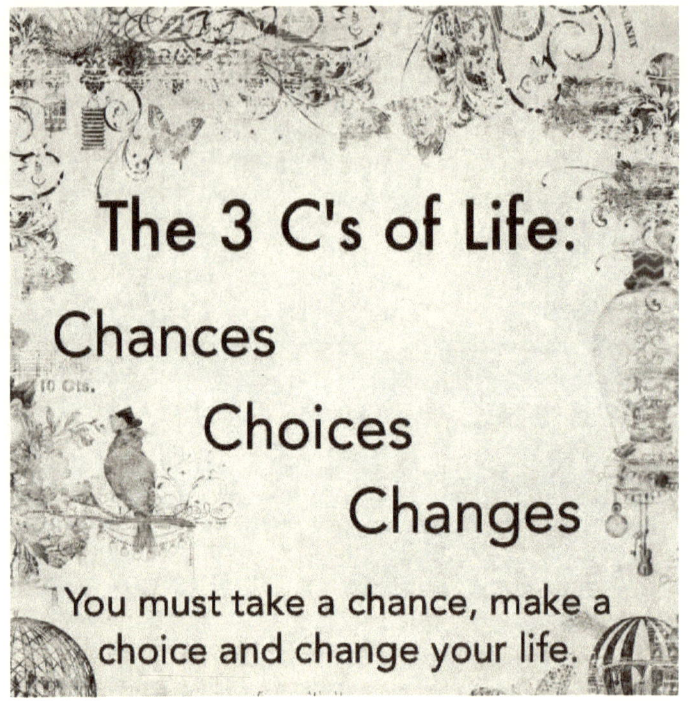

The 3 C's of Life:
Chances
Choices
Changes
You must take a chance, make a
choice and change your life.

Some people think that to be strong is to never feel pain. In reality, the strongest people are the ones who feel it, understand it, accept and learn from it.

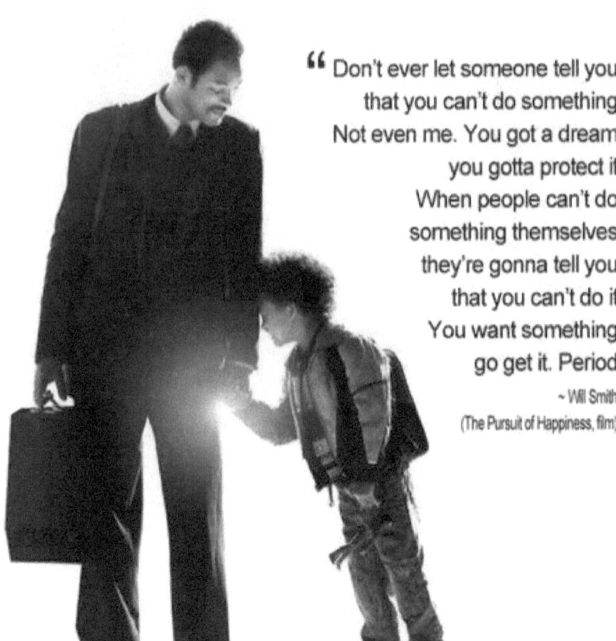
Don't ever let someone tell you
that you can't do something.
Not even me. You got a dream,
you gotta protect it.
When people can't do
something themselves,
they're gonna tell you
that you can't do it.
You want something,
go get it. Period.
~ Will Smith
(The Pursuit of Happiness, film)

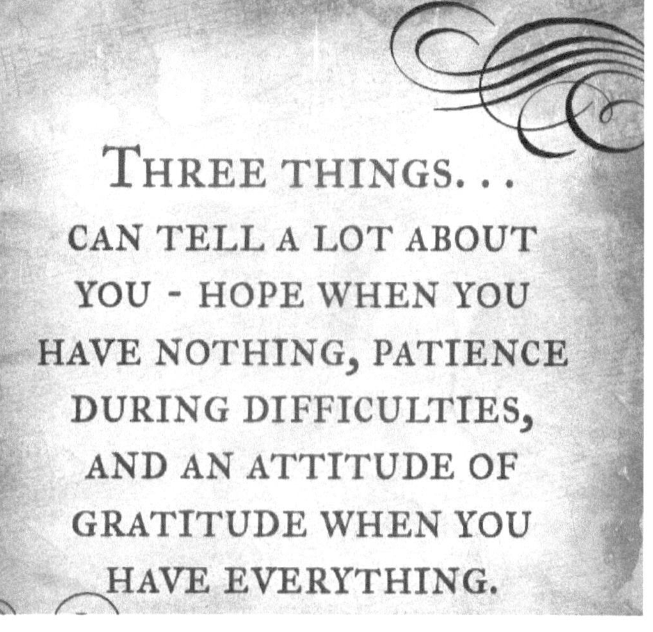
THREE THINGS...
CAN TELL A LOT ABOUT
YOU - HOPE WHEN YOU
HAVE NOTHING, PATIENCE
DURING DIFFICULTIES,
AND AN ATTITUDE OF
GRATITUDE WHEN YOU
HAVE EVERYTHING.

True love
isn't always
romantic...
It's a choice to love each
other for better or worse,
richer or poorer, and in
sickness or health.

Two things to remember in life.
Take care of your thoughts
when you are alone,
and take care of your words
when you are with people.

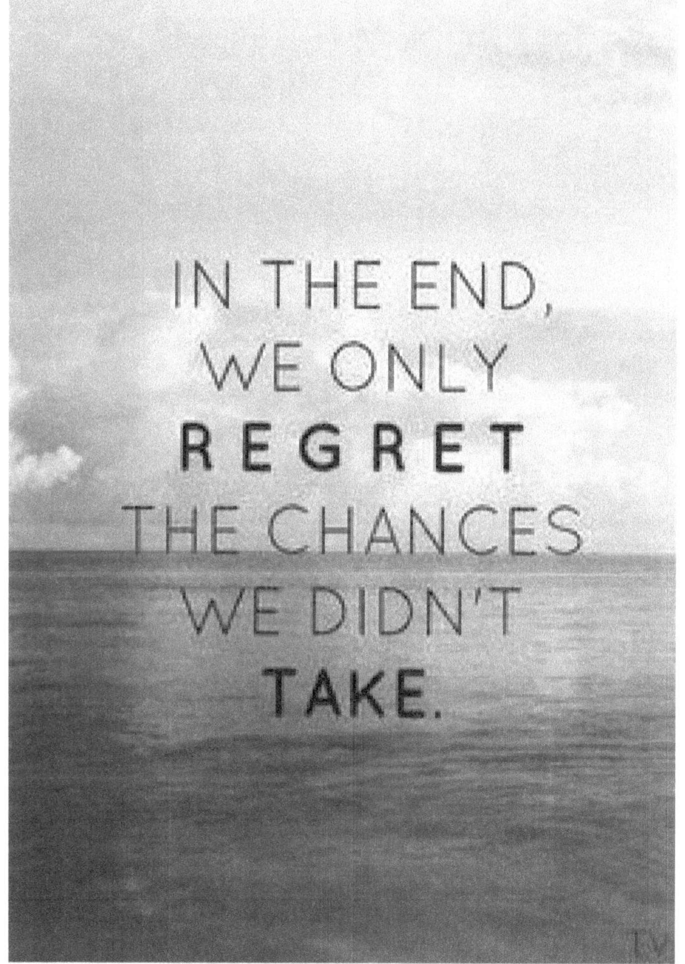
IN THE END,
WE ONLY
REGRET
THE CHANCES
WE DIDN'T
TAKE.

I AM STRONG, BECAUSE I'VE BEEN WEAK.
I AM FEARLESS, BECAUSE I'VE BEEN AFRAID.
I AM WISE, BECAUSE I'VE BEEN FOOLISH.

"THE WORLD AIN'T ALL SUNSHINE AND RAINBOWS.
IT'S A VERY MEAN AND NASTY PLACE,
AND I DON'T CARE HOW TOUGH YOU ARE,
IT WILL BEAT YOU TO YOUR KNEES
AND KEEP YOU THERE PERMANENTLY IF YOU LET IT.
YOU, ME OR NOBODY IS GONNA HIT AS HARD AS LIFE.
BUT IT AIN'T ABOUT HOW HARD YOU HIT,
IT'S ABOUT HOW HARD YOU CAN GET HIT
AND KEEP MOVING FORWARD.
HOW MUCH YOU CAN TAKE AND KEEP MOVING FORWARD.
THAT'S HOW WINNING IS DONE!"
-ROCKY BALBOA

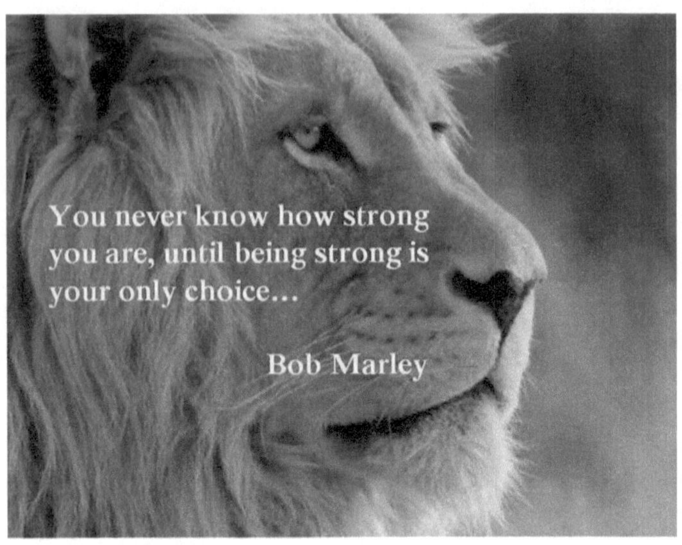
You never know how strong
you are, until being strong is
your only choice...

Bob Marley

"If she's amazing, she won't be easy. If she's easy, she won't be amazing. If she's worth it, you won't give up. If you give up, you're not worthy. ... Truth is, everybody is going to hurt you; you just gotta find the ones worth suffering for."
Bob Marley

Mankind must put an end to war,
or war will put an end to mankind.

John F. Kennedy

"We live in a world where we have
to hide to make love,
while violence is practiced
in broad daylight."

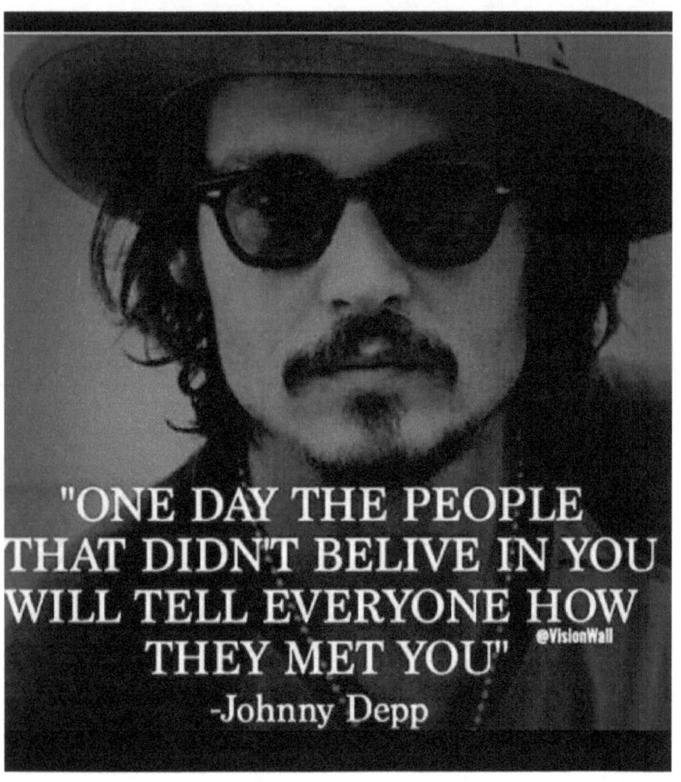

"ONE DAY THE PEOPLE
THAT DIDN'T BELIVE IN YOU
WILL TELL EVERYONE HOW
THEY MET YOU"
@VisionWall
-Johnny Depp

Being nice to someone
you dislike doesn't
mean you're fake.
It means you are mature
enough to tolerate your
dislike towards them.

FAMOUS FAILURES

ALBERT EINSTEIN

He wasn't able to speak until he was almost 4-years-old and his teachers said he would "never amount to much"

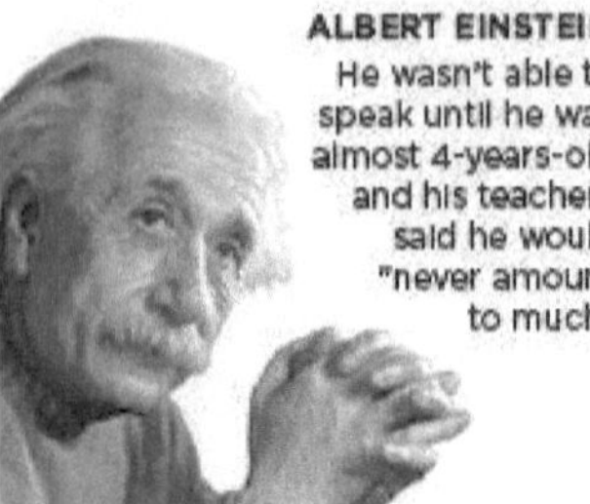

MICHAEL JORDAN

After being cut from his high school basketball team, he went home, locked himself in his room, and cried.

WALT DISNEY

Fired from a newspaper for "lacking imagination" and "having no original ideas."

STEVE JOBS

At 30-years-old he was left devastated and depressed after being unceremoniously removed from the company he started.

OPRAH WINFREY

Was demoted from her job as a news anchor because she "wasn't fit for television."

THE BEATLES

Rejected by Decca Recording Studios, who said "We don't like their sound—they have no future in show business."

IF YOU'VE NEVER FAILED,
YOU'VE NEVER TRIED ANYTHING NEW

"I walk slowly,
but I never walk
backward."

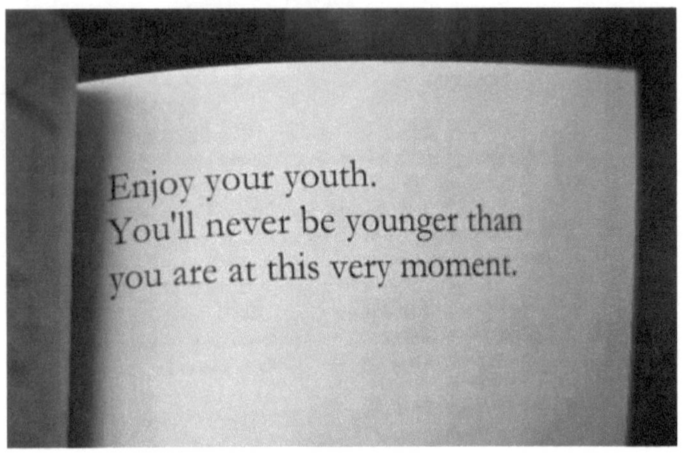
Enjoy your youth.
You'll never be younger than
you are at this very moment.

CHICAGOFITFREAK.TUMBLR.COM
IT'S YOUR ROAD
& YOUR'S ALONE.
OTHERS MAY WALK IT WITH YOU,
BUT NO ONE CAN WALK IT FOR YOU.

SUCCESS IS NO ACCIDENT.
It is hard work, perseverance,
learning, studying, sacrifice
and most of all, love of what you are doing.
- Pele

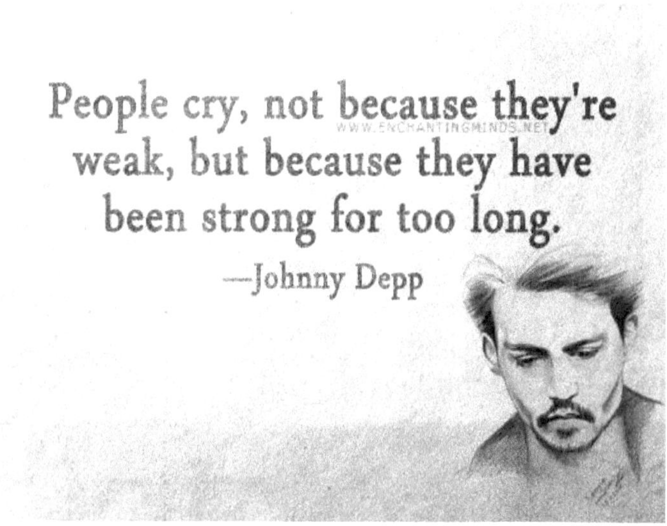
People cry, not because they're weak, but because they have been strong for too long.
—Johnny Depp
WWW.ENCHANTINGMINDS.NET

Difficult
doesnt
mean
impossible.

It simply means
that you have
to work hard.

"A person who never made a mistake never tried anything new."

— Albert Einstein

I've missed more than
9,000 shots in my career.
I've lost almost 300 games.
26 times I've been trusted to
take the game winning
shot and missed.
I've failed over and over and over
again in my life and
that is why I Succeed.
- Michael Jordan

No One
Rises Suddenly
In The World,
Not Even
The Sun

Every great dream begins with a dreamer. Always remember, you have within you the strength, the patience, and the passion to reach for the stars to change the world.
-Harriet Tubman-

It is not only for what we do that we are held responsible, but also for what we do not do.

- Moliere

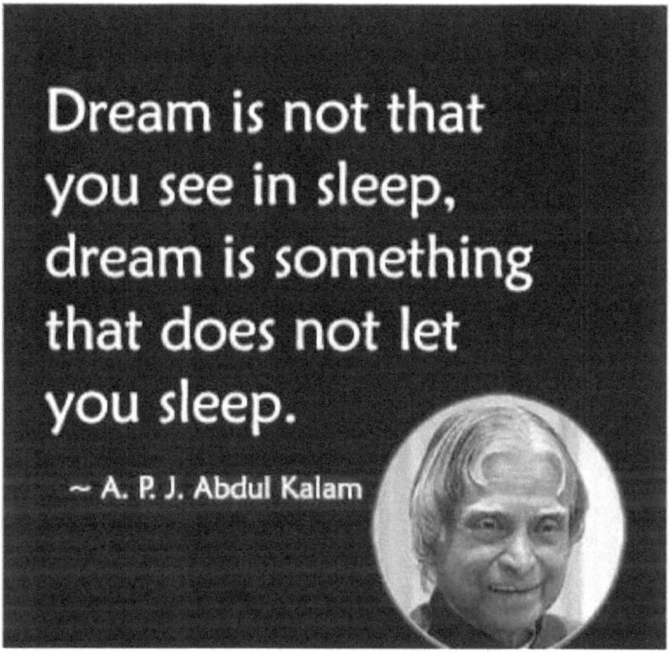

Dream is not that
you see in sleep,
dream is something
that does not let
you sleep.
~ A. P. J. Abdul Kalam

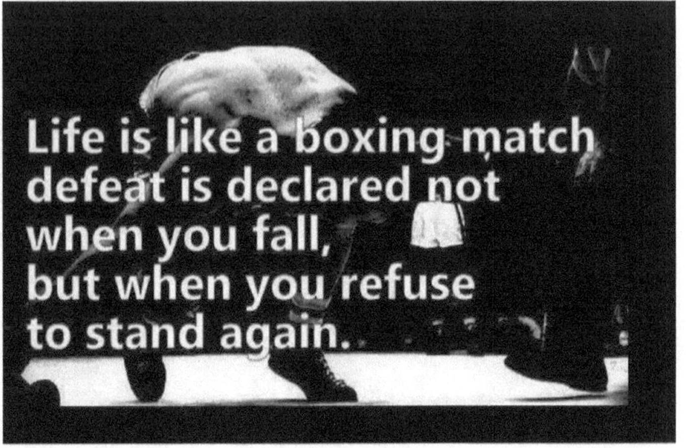
Life is like a boxing match
defeat is declared not
when you fall,
but when you refuse
to stand again.

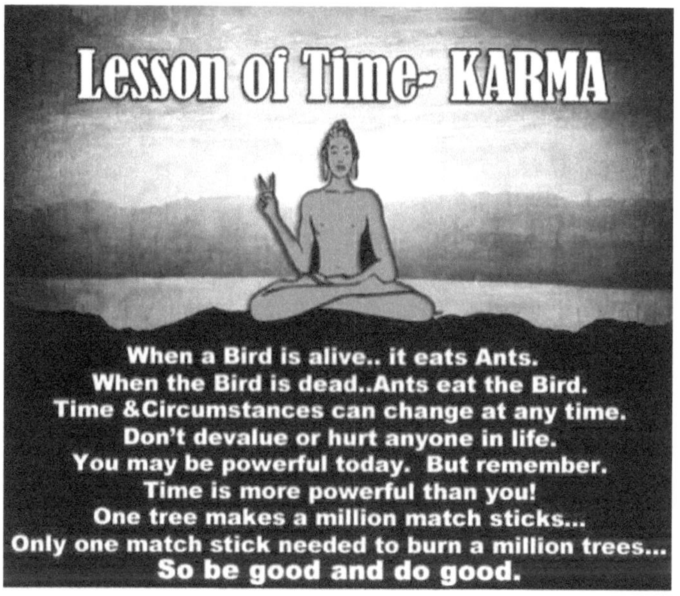
Lesson of Time- KARMA
When a Bird is alive.. it eats Ants.
When the Bird is dead..Ants eat the Bird.
Time &Circumstances can change at any time.
Don't devalue or hurt anyone in life.
You may be powerful today. But remember.
Time is more powerful than you!
One tree makes a million match sticks...
Only one match stick needed to burn a million trees...
So be good and do good.

Marlon Brando: Content People

"Too many people are content to get by, to wait and to see what might happen. These are dying people. Sad people. If I were a better man, a wiser man, a younger man, I would go out and try to get these people to believe in things again; to fight the easy way, the sad way, and really do something with their talents and their loves and their lives."—Marlon Brando interview with James Grissom

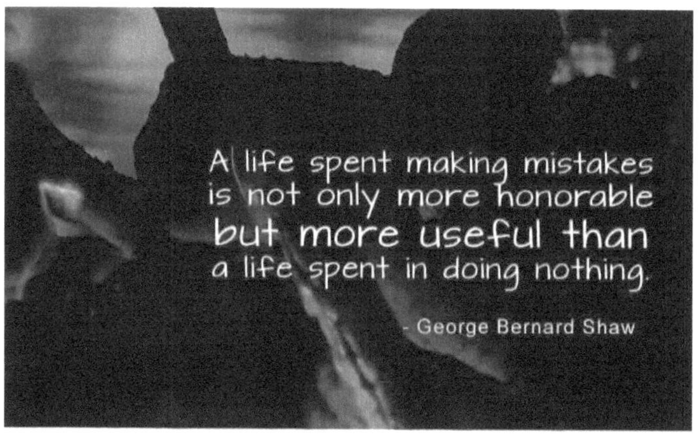
A life spent making mistakes
is not only more honorable
but more useful than
a life spent in doing nothing.
- George Bernard Shaw

Don't be afraid of
death;
Be afraid of an
unlived life.
You don't have to
live forever,
You just have to
live.

SOME OF MY FAVORITE QUOTES RIGHT HERE FROM **ONE TREE HILL** ARE BELOW:

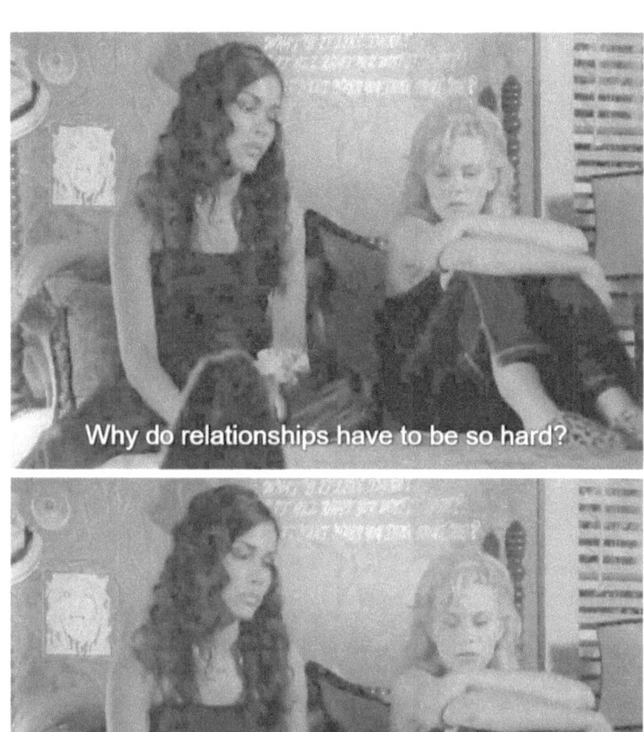
Why do relationships have to be so hard?
Because the only thing harder is being alone.

I want to believe
in it all again —

Music and art,
fate and love.

And i want to believe
that i've made the right choices

And that i'm
on the right path

And there's still time
to fix the mistakes i've made.

And i guess i want hope.

life isn't fair, clay.
but you being miserable
is never gonna change that.

Robert Louis Stevenson wrote:
"YOU CAN NOT RUN AWAY FROM WEAKNESS; YOU MUST FIGHT IT OUT...
OR PERISH. AND IF THAT BE SO, WHY NOT NOW, AND WHERE YOU STAND?"
@ONLYOTH
EP:3x08

Sometimes I think we waste our words
and we waste our moments

And we don't take the time to say the things
that are in our hearts when we have the chance

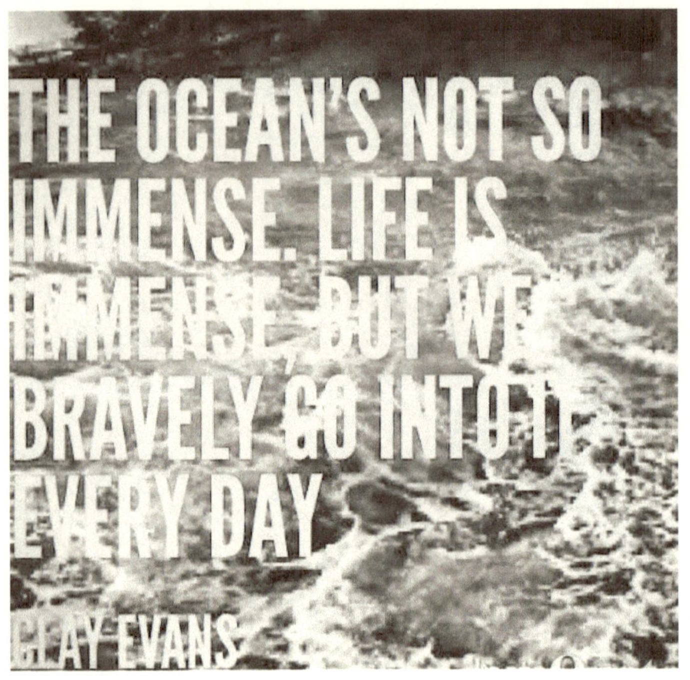

THE OCEAN'S NOT SO
IMMENSE. LIFE IS
IMMENSE, BUT WE
BRAVELY GO INTO IT
EVERY DAY
CLAY EVANS

It doesn't matter how you plan it.
It doesn't matter how you envision it.
Without even knowing it, sometimes life has a way of finding
you with exactly what you need. Or exactly who you need.

The hardest part of saying goodbye
Is having to do it again every single day.
Every day, we face the same truth
That life is fleeting.
SPORTS
RAVENS TO RETIRE QUENTIN FIELDS' NUMBER
That our time here is short.
And to honor the fallen.
We must live our own lives well.

Every night,
I sing songs about love.
And then I sit on my bus
and I write songs about love.
And the only thing
I really know about love
is that it's unknowable.

Yeah, well, the truth is,
I'm not sure I've been
thatracious about any of it
you're still here, aren't you,
still finding your way?
That's about as much
grace as anyone can ask.

But... I mean, if you're always looking
for reasons not to be with somebody,
then you'll always find them.
And, I guess, at some point,
maybe you should let go and...
give your heart what it deserves.

"Sometimes it's easy to feel like you're the only one in the world who's struggling,
"who's frustrated or unsatisfied or barely getting by."
"But that feeling's a lie.
"And if you just hold on,
"just find the courage to face it all for another day,
"someone or something will find you and make it all okay.

"Because we all need
a little help sometimes.
"Someone to help us
hear the music in the world,
"to remind us
that it won't always be this way. "
And that someone will find you."
"That someone is out there.

Quotes   from *The   Queen's   Gambit*-   Netflix
Original:Below

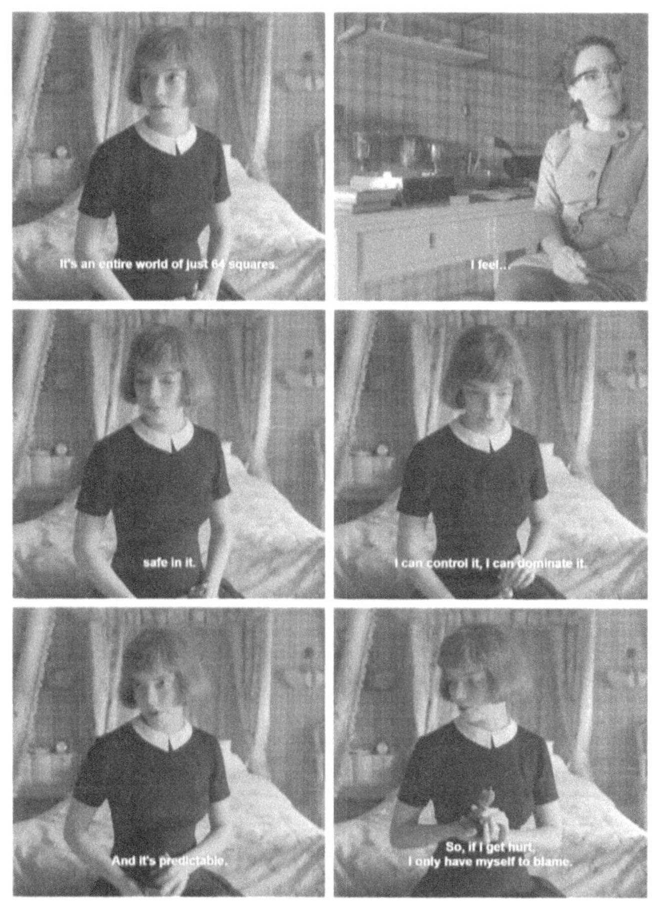
It's an entire world of just 64 squares.
I feel...
safe in it.
I can control it, I can dominate it.
And it's predictable.
So, if I get hurt,
I only have myself to blame.

Quotes And Sayings By Me

1- Food, water & oxygen keep us alive but, Art makes us feel alive. - Urvashi Sinha

2- Greatness comes by doing the good things in a great way - Urvashi Sinha

3- Have you once had something, which you don't have anymore but you are willing to do almost anything to have that back in your life so that you will not have to lose what you have again! - Urvashi Sinha

4- People who get to live the dream, live the life too... but people who get to live the life.. don't necessarily get to live their dreams too. -Urvashi Sinha

5- That's the thing I like about things, that things remain but people leave. - Urvashi Sinha

6- Life is like a fill-in-the-blanks, we have been given a sheet of paper called life, and the fillers are the family in which we get born, our mind and body. Sometimes we get confused about what to fill in the blanks given, those blanks are opportunities and circumstances. What we need to do is to fill in all the blanks in the right manner! - Urvashi Sinha

7- Every day I wake up and my mind says, I should be thankful to god and life because I have eyes, ears, voice, some food on my plate, a roof over my head, and most importantly I am breathing. But for the heart, it is not enough! It is easy to say these things to the mind, but difficult to teach the heart the same. - Urvashi Sinha

8- Lately, I have realized that to dream of something and to take the responsibility for that dream are two different things altogether. Not everyone who dares to dream something big could be able to take the responsibility for what and how much it takes and demands. It could be hard work, self-discipline, and sacrifices as well! - Urvashi Sinha

9- After seeing bad times in life we should become strong-hearted, and not stone-hearted. - Urvashi Sinha

Zindagi mein bura waqt dekhne ke baad humein Mazboot Dil banna chahiye, Patthar Dil (Insensitive) nhn!
- Urvashi Sinha

10- In this world, everyone is trying to become something rather than knowing that are they also becoming good human beings! To become big is not a very big thing but to become a great human being is a huge thing. Try to become a good human being before becoming anything else. - Urvashi Sinha

Duniya mein har insaan kuch na kuch banne ki jugat mein laga hua hai..ye bina jaane ki kya wo acha insaan b ban pa raha hai. Kisi ne bahut khoob kaha hai ki bada banna itni badi baat nhn..par acha insaan banna bahut badi baat hai. Zindagi mein kuch b banne se pahle ik ache insaan bano...!
- Urvashi Sinha

11- Foreverness in relationships, feelings, and emotions is one of the greatest things ever. otherwise, nowadays temporariness is all around from LED bulbs to everything. - Urvashi Sinha

Feelings aur relations mein forever ki baat hi kuch aur hoti hai...baaki temporary to aajkal LED bulb se leke sab kuch hai !

\- Urvashi Sinha

12- Without art my life is nothing, I am nothing - Urvashi Sinha

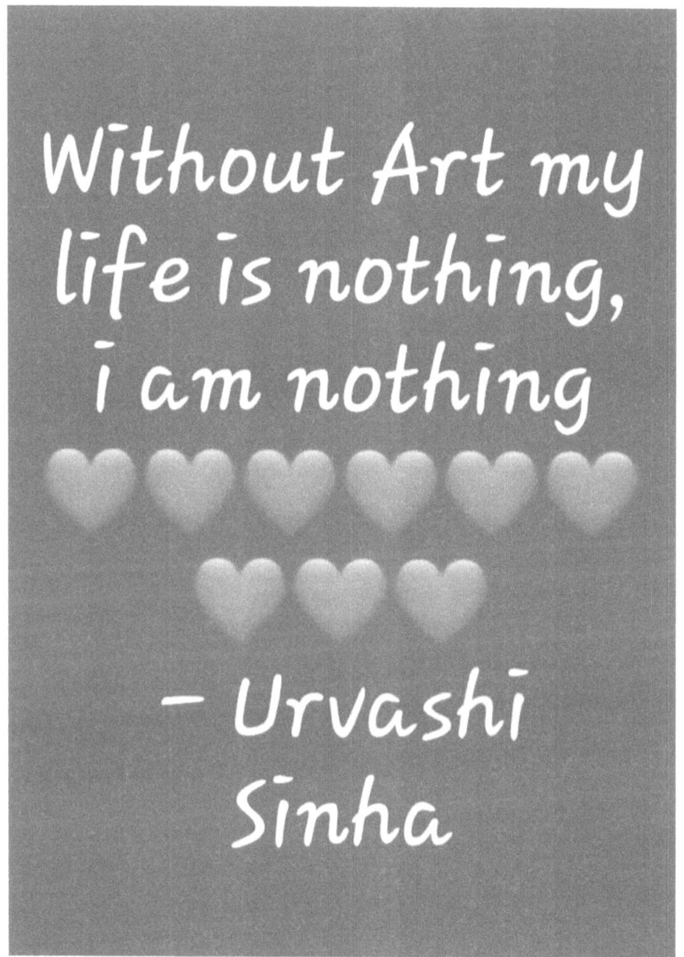

*13- I can't understand how some people can live
without dreams & passion! because for me these are*

like heart & breath. dreams and hopes are like oxygen. - Urvashi Sinha

like heart & breath. dreams and hopes are like oxygen. - Urvashi Sinha

I can't understand how some people can live without Dreams & Passion ! Bcz for me these are like heart & breathe 💟 💟 Dreams and hopes are like oxygen

— Urvashi Sinha

14- Dreamers (especially artists) & Aashiqs don't get sleep easily at night! The moral of the story is if you get to sleep easily every night, then you are not in love with anyone or anything. life is nothing without love and passion. - Urvashi Sinha

Dreamers (spsly Artists) & Aashiqs doesn't get sleep easily at night! Moral of the story– if u get sleep easily everyday then u r not in love with anyone or anything 🤍🤍 and life is nothing without love and passion.

– Urvashi Sinha

15- It hurts like hell when someone leaves you, but it hurts tragically.. when someone leaves you without leaving! - Urvashi Sinha

16- Sometimes people say things they don't mean, and sometimes people mean some things so well but don't say it.   - Urvashi Sinha

17- Moral of the life is that story is short, write it in the best way possible! - Urvashi Sinha

18- The thing is that I always have been serious with my life, but I am waiting for my life to be serious with me. - Urvashi Sinha

19- In childhood we make the bed wet, after getting older we make the pillow wet.   - Urvashi Sinha

All the above quotes and sayings are written by me! I hope all the readers enjoyed it.

By concluding this book I would like to say thanks to

some of the teachers of my life so far: ONE TREE HILL, Movies, Music & My Soul.